# DANCES IN THE THEATER OF THE MIND

by

## ROBERT C. SAUNDERS

Dynamically Activated, LLC

# What people are saying about
## *Dances in the Theater of the Mind*

"Robert's words create a thoughtful space so desperately needed in a world carelessly cluttered with the chaos of our everyday."

Chris Steinocher, President & CEO
St. Petersburg Area Chamber of Commerce

"These poems are marked and smoothed by an intrinsic dignity and it makes my hair stand on end at its originality."

Ndipmong Inyang, Entrepreneur

"Funny, heartwarming and intelligent, this collection of upbeat poems of love and the lighter side of life reflects not only the author's personality, it reveals an image of how most people want to view the world. A truly enjoyable read."

Jennifer Thayer, Smith & Associates Real Estate

"These inspiring poems of Mr. Saunders play upon the strings of the heart, addressing the full range of human emotions in its own unique way."

Susan J. Rouzer, Florida Direct Cremation and Burial Society

"These words invoke the thoughts that others would be motivated to apply to their lasting benefit. Definitely soul-searching words worth reading over and over again."

Winston Goulbourne, Retired transmission repairman

## DANCES IN THE THEATER OF THE MIND

Book cover design by Bayprint

Photograph provided by Vanessa Protic of Demure-Lynn Photography

Published by:
Dynamically Activated LLC
304 37th Ave N
Suite 310
St. Petersburg, FL 33704
dynamicallyactivated@gmail.com

Visit the author website:
www.robertcsaunders.com
www.dynamicallyactivated.com

ISBN: 978-0-9982692-3-8 (eBook)
ISBN: 978-0-9982692-7-6 (Paperback)

POETRY/GENERAL

Version 2018.05.10

This book is dedicated to my parents,

Victor Emmanuel Saunders:
January 25th, 1937 – October 29th, 2016

Gloria Bernice Saunders:
April 3rd, 1937 – May 2nd, 2017

They always desired that all seven children reach their full potential and I am ever grateful for it.

Very special thanks to:

Bayprint for book cover design;

Vanessa Protic of Demure-Lynn Photography for cover
photographs;

Jaqueline Dobbs for initial typing and proof reading;

Nursing Instructor Catherine Crumb for always demanding
more of me than I demanded of myself.

# OTHER BOOKS

# BY

# ROBERT C. SAUNDERS

Nurses Bred for Business:
*The Awakening Of Legions Of Nurse Entrepreneurs*

Foodie Dessertations:
*Bite Sized Recipes Of Foodielicious Poetry*

Rythmic Elegance:
*A poetic treatise on our place in the universe*

# TABLE OF CONTENTS

# PREFACE

It has not been that long ago that I took ballroom dance lessons. I had a blast and took copious notes as I was determined to understand the theory, the practice, the science, the art, and the pageantry of dance. What quickly arose on my dance journey is that dancing emerged as expression of humans living, loving and experiencing life itself! It can invoke warlike hostility, promote team solidarity, reveal happiness or stir romantic passion. You may have noted in your own experience that dancing can reveal marital unity or discord. It's sad when couples don't dance together anymore, in more ways than one. I don't think it's a coincidence dancing is universally integral to every major societal function were music is involved. Hence, life itself is a dance that must be properly choreographed in the theater of unspoken rhythms. Each of us then, must study, observe and, as perfectly as possible, practice the proper steps. Don't hesitate to acquire the proper knowledge and coaching as "All" of the dance greats had coaches. We must also continue to develop an ear for music, especially good music that motivates us to get up and get into the dance, in synch with the best moments and opportunities that life has to offer. What follows are a series of poetic "Acts" that each of us may have played roles in throughout our life either as a dancer, choreographer or spectator. Three, two, one...and... ACTION!!!!

# ACT I

Hope, Faith and Love

# Caught Wealthy

Surprise! Caught in the moment endearment
rendered in rich embraces. A trove of good
graces. Strip mined pleasant thoughts, golden
faces. Vast landscapes of tenderness pastures.

Heaping doses of warmth, feelings beautiful
in granduers. For surety in a loveless world
if one has these they are truly blest a lasting
pleasure.

Thus, secure such ample supplies of needed
support and feeling are well protected as
hidden treasure.

Before others find and take advantage of
your fantastic intangibles in full measure.

# Ascending

Rose of romantic elation plucked from
the conscience is slated. For the one whose
heart shapes love in such outpourings unabated.
Thoughts of fancy take flight.

Light and free riding the waves of emotion, a
kite. Striving along in the beauty of the day
that melts into the night.

Run, runs indeed thru my soul like a cheetah
on a roll. My life, my desire meets you as
now two unique people is made into the
whole ... Ascending.

# Love

Is it any wonder every human at distant and
recent past prospered from strength to strength
in its abundance, and abased to exist when family
units lost loves thriving dynamic and resilient
substance.

In the present time continuum of human destiny,
people living without it is never to be, won't be
replaced by super advances in technology.

Forever will it remain the favored topic of
stimulating talk show fair, enquiring minds
unceasingly curious as to how to navigate
thru the challenges love's peculiarities bring to bear.

Musically inclined voices produce top notes that
broche the subjects every nuance and most subtle
shade, It's the cement of which eternally happy,
peaceful marriages are made.

Sexuality is loves beautifully expressed

1 / 5

serendipitous side effect, that encompasses
tenderness and unselfish giving that two enjoined
would work hard to protect.

Out of this union sprouts the birth of new life and
new love thriving, at death love does not die but
continues burning forever in the hearts and minds
of those whom hope dwell and keeps on striving.

This great power is also what makes divorce so
painful when endured, as it involves ripping apart
two souls with one heart shared once
permanently sealed and insured.

One party or the other love's virtues abandoned
no longer desiring them to be explored love is
what you make it to be, the romance novel or the
tragedy, hell on earth or blissful majesty,
It's the greatest adventure running the gambit of
human thought and nativity.

When distilled it summarizes what we are now
and all we can and ever will be, Intangible
in principle descending from above, superlative,
divine, and dynamic .... this thing called love.

# Emotion

Emotion conjured from the depths of human
psyche, a beast who dictates never to be tamed
by logic's discipline, shrinking of reason's civility.

It's biting and ripping to shreds rationality's
thoughtful response, why such a beast exists
except to add color to consciousness shading the
gray with white resonance.

Adding to darkness all that can be made bright,
gives motivation to begin a task that gives birth
to curious insight.

With its endless questions that never stop being
asked, the source of dream's, visions and goals
pushing us forward to task.

As one human kind we will see what the future
holds, and as long as existence beckons we can
invite what unfolds.

All that is worth human striving and undertaking

will remain rough with a great deal of risk, since emotions respond to the past the present runs brisk.

In the here and now, in anticipation of future excitatory notions, it will forever remain the untamed animal that got away without seconding that emotion.

# Frame of mind

Tempered cool in sudden contemplations
of the problematic forces in nature I'm
humbled by the realization of my smallness
in endless space, the astrophysical quandary
of mental meandering race.

Unencumbered afire, with new ideas vividly
pulsing thru a panorama of old times and new
places, pleasant smiles and unforgettable faces,
memories colored by experience shaped by force
of will perceptions framed by the boundaries of
knowledge and ignorance paces.

At once a snapshot of time immemorial, hung as
a picture on the walls of personal achievement, a
legacy sign, to be posted on as a cherished
moment to fondly remembered, nestled, and
framed of mind.

# You are the better part of my whole life

My affection for you devoid of obtrusive ulterior
connotations, infatuation fixations remand,
intangible feelings in me that can move
mountains lofty and grand.

Upon which my love solid and affirmed for you
on unsinkable ground unrequited, for all to see
that each day each moment that I learn more
about you I'm committed.

More and more to preserve this precious bond
well outfitted, evenly yoked in spirit in goals, in
personality, meshed together thoughts and hearts
properly knitted.

Love so deep and unconditional that will stand
the test of time, two, yes, we against the world
certainly pitted your words dear inspired from the
start, you know my weaknesses and frailties yet
you have drawn closer to me instead of apart, for
this I extol you queen in my life, enthroned in my

heart, you woman inspire greatness, strength,
self-confidence you impart, vast are the treasures
in your midst true beauty in form, a
masterful wonder of priceless art.

No man could want more or desire less in a wife,
this is what makes you the better part of my
whole life.

# The
# dilemma

"0" that mice like men should become
man of virtue. That noble women could respect
not deny them. Then, only emasculated men and
mice, like women, would decry them.

# The well-watered wife

All husbands should have a green thumb,
to till the soul of marriage and plant his wife in
wisdom.

One would shower her with loving concern, the
very thing that time should cause men to discern.

Special attention is necessary to pour out as
special is she, calls her honest appraisal of the
soil that is weed and bug free.

She can't remain potted forever, her roots must
grow deeper with time and strong endeavor.

Shower her with beautiful expressions that'll
make her a keeper of kind words and as such, his
strong lead will only make her flourish stately by
gentle touch.

Deeds of compassion and forgiveness will

fertilize emotional resolve, let her bask in the
light of demonstrated love.

This is the stuff of gentility, that will open and
release the soft fragrance and beauty that
defines femininity.

No emotional rough housing and a low stress
simple life, that is what will make for a content
and well-watered wife.

# Shared by two

Heart to heart two beats sound of one love
true, deeper than the sea can be shaded with
greater height than skies have blue.

Stretching into eternity's expanse that eyes can't
see, demystifying emotional complexities.
sees the forest for the trees, proposes blessed
spiritual union on bended knees.

Stars twinkle bright forever telling of what
endearment between two souls can do,
universal harmony bespeaking the power of one
love's heart shared by two.

# Beautiful black woman

Comeliness of skin characterizes dignified
virtues, thick, elegant locks grow from a
foundation that strong qualities imbues.

To a Nubian queen of eminent repose, soft and
mild resplendence of a regal juxtapose.

Royalty is her birth right as exemplified in
elegant gait, her majesty strong African roots
recount and story tellers jubilate.

Intelligence and wisdom is her scepter relished,
understanding and peace typifies her crown of
beauty detailed and embellished.

She anoints her peers with oils of compassion and
endears all to her in compelling respectful, like
fashion.

Success will be the throne this one occupies
due to her acknowledging those greater and
coming on them to reckon.

With a heart of discernment is how she'll reign
supreme, with dignity and eminence by her side
her household will beam, with such power and
personality no wonder you're an appreciative
man's dream.

# Chocolate thoughts

Her words, creamy eaten up after each wise
utterance, swallowed smoothly as positivity
is what is bestowed richly upon my soul, hair
flowing as a tasteful river, velvety textured,
appreciated persuasive as a whole.

Grace and tact she always employs,
exhibiting the light flavor of manners and
forms, angelic sweet, a natural treat to enjoy.

The words she doesn't say but body and eyes
bespeak a euphoric mindscape as it taunts, a
taste sensation formed by feminine repose
turning chocolate thoughts.

# Mathematically divined

She one plus he one is love number crunched
infinitely cool and calculated, a common denominator
of happiness estimated and long awaited.

Her smile evokes the subtotal of a key emotional
equation, the end product extrapolated to the female
persuasion, her lips speak statistically curvaceous
intimation, correlated in principles, captured by reason,
arrested by smooth algebraic intonations.

Her eyes divine the square root of my being profound
anew, exponential possibilities in this life that I'm
seeing, I times you makes infinity true.

# Ballroom dance lessons

Intelligent, discreet, most patient and kind,
like a sought after hidden treasure another
Instructor like her would be hard to find.

Insightful of note, most interesting style teaching,
proper techniques by rote, centered poise she is
beseeching.

All students to reach out beyond present limitation,
perfect practice makes perfect for crowd pleasing
presentation.

Heel then toe to floor to express deep gratitude, for
your hard work as teacher's appreciation I
exude.

Fred Astaire and Ginger Rogers would be proud of their
legacy a true dance nation, so bring a guest and dance
shoes in tow and continue to taste the sensation.

My candy

Never knew sweet things could Nestle Crunch
me until the Reese's of my lonely heart came
Across a Bit *O* Honey walking thru the door.

*Twix* graceful form, inspired beauty she exist
to captivate me, Twizzlers a whirl in my head.
Have I beheld such a vision in a movie?
On the silver screen ... Uh whatchamacallit? ...

Starring some Kit Kat. Oh Henry! that I may play
the leading role in her life a ... 3 Musketeers
winning the sweet affection of her Hershey's
Hugs and Kisses.

An astronaut traveling the Milky Way's of
love, this is serious! Nothing to Snickers at.
Just call me *Mr.* Goodbar after our lover's
spat.

We'll marry, happily tasting the wedded bliss of
*York* Peppermint Patties. We'll move to $5^{th}$ Avenue
and have lots of *M&M's* ... indeed life with a loved
one is what you make of it, plain or a little nutty.
Either it will melt in your mouth or melt in your hands.
It's up to you what you do with ... *your* candy.

## The precious things in life

What do you treasure most in life? What will each of us
hold precious when the chips are down and life is
burdened with strife? Will strife keep stealing material
aspirations and bankrupting hopes and dreams robbed
with cold realities knife?

What matters most is what can't be bought, as
it is those intangibles that are most priceless and
endlessly sought.

One should hold in high regard the diamonds of love most
precious in its varied luster, expressive qualities,
immeasurable for weight holding families together in
fiery muster.

Continue exhibiting sapphires of understanding
sure to please keep digging for rubies of insight,
that will see one thru the toughest challenges and
pearls of affection to warm the heart on the
coldest night.

Examine the amethyst of caring attention to convey

tenderness in the most caring way, collect the onyx of
time to be spent upon higher spiritual priorities that
infinitely matter most today.

Garner jades of joy felt in having satisfying intimate
living, relationships with chrysolite of appreciation
expressed in the moment and never slips in gathering with
topaz of thanksgiving.

For a wealth of health and family and duality caused by
pearls of wisdom rife, leading to a deep and abiding
contentment these things, yes, only these
are truly the precious things in life.

# Inspiration

Deep driving forces, elevating sources, from the depths of being creative, elative and relative to all that humans define and success endorses.

Some are moved by principles whispered from our past, culled from our present and righteous participles shaping our future, still others are compelled by people and the theoretical precepts they represent or sacred scripture these adhere to.

Whomever we are moved by, wherever they may be in the grand scheme of inspiration, and whatever it takes to help us along the path of discovery, keep breathing in eternal universal truths, continue clearing a path of personal discover and hold such dear as nothing can be brought to bear on us to succeed as the ascending effects of inspiration.

# Stop and smell the roses

Strong fragrances beckon a soul bestirred by
appreciation for silken dainty roses massaged by the
intimate affections of morning dew, petals opening
with smiling faces blushing magenta, orange, red in
varying hue.

Pleasant thought flurries, elated hearts glowing,
cleansing troubled expressions defiled by the day's
worries.

Phenomenal are the effects of silent sentinels waving
its motionless wet eyes, rooted marches across
earth's fields stretching to the heavens ever seeking
approval of dew drenched skies.

Well coifed every day in Sunday's best, ostentatious
yet without pride, so priceless in serving curious
smelling noses, loud in silent song, compelling one
and all passing by to stop and smell the roses.

# Smile

A thought of love, a deed of the heart rationed,
imprinted by the swath of enduring passion.

Started from the moment that like and friend became
I love you, smiles signaling this lover will always
stay true.

The light shining from the soul's lantern piercing the
face of beauteous reality style, rendered and most
often engendered in a warm, magnetic, stirring smile.

# World Full of Happy Faces

Look! Brilliant sunshine caressing millions of happy
radiant faces like open books, living in happifying
circumstances with joyous mental outlooks.

Clean consciences, clean hearts serene, no more
entrapped by dictates of sin or evil intent, everyone
working toward a righteous bent.

As there is one standard of justice, for all have
decided, so glad that no unprincipled ideologies exist
to keep men divided.

No derisive religions to alienate men, confuse minds
and hide the free gifts of ultimate truth from sincere
hearts, human souls, now unencumbered by Adam's
sin can tap and attain unlimited potentials inherent,
great appreciation by all will be heir apparent in all its
parts.

Everyone stands to take advantage of Christ's
example of willing self sacrifice and obedience to all
tenets that his father Jehovah commands, whose will
is that mankind's ultimate destiny written in
eternities boundlessness demands.

Mandating that in a future of divine shaping all
humble souls will enjoy the promise mortgage free
places, forever living out the desire of every human
in a world full of happy faces.

# Best things in life are free

Your $1,000 dollar hugs silkily wrap me in its
luxuriant silver trappings, $20,000 dollar whispers
from your palate shimmer in my mind as fine gold
wrappings.

Cannot hide the need to hold you as rare kingly
treasure sought and finally embraced, your $500,000
dollar kisses rush the senses heavenly graced.

$1,000,000 carat moments spent with you slide thru
diamond studded thoughts multifaceted in ways
beatific, with $1,000,000,000 dollar platinum
qualities most desirable and specific.

You are to have and to hold appreciatively, in
sickness and in wealth, knowing that your priceless
love has been finally found by me to exchange
abundantly.

It is true, the best things in life are absolutely free.

# Love has everything to do with it

What's love got to do with anything? Everyone
should live as one wants, do as one pleases you say?
Say whatever you like without regard to
consequences? How selfish!

Sexually transmitted diseases, pregnant teens, broken
families, shattered hopes and dreams.

Cry, indeed, plead for love properly expressed,
gainfully applied, appropriately addressed.

Ultraviolent ethnic cleansing, spiritual, political,
economic, physical slavery burgeon in a loveless
soup of dark personal agendas extending.

All such immoral psychosis proliferating and
derisive, all who feed upon it can only become
exceedingly divisive.

Self interest parading as genuine concern,

depravedly self serving, at a time when untold
masses of humanity suffer in impunity unnerving.

Loving kindness, spiritual mindedness, conformity to
a universal constitution mandating love administered
as a humane wish.

What if sincerity of heart was popularly chosen as a
way of life championing humility of mind, real
concern for others in abundance without brevity?
most difficult to find!

Moral excellence of character and self accountability
could team well with willing full personal
responsibility.

Indeed, I beg to differ, multidimensional love has
everything to do with it.

# Thief in the night

Steadily she creeps stealthily through a black
velvet star studded veneer characterizing
my nights shaded with cool contemplations
of class and gentililty.

Unlocking the safe of emotional barriers held secure
in my days of alertness to feminine guile and
effeminate wile.

Now lost to soft calculating mascara eyes, melting
away inhibitions by way of sway and kilter, how can
she steal anything with shapely thighs? Hmmm!

Famous last words! As she already stole my heart!
Men may dominate in the wee hours, or so I thought
underestimating female powers.

How do I get my heart back from someone so
mesmerizing? Where would I start to look? Should I
start to look? Should I care that I was not more

careful? She did it without my putting up a fight,

What skill! What cunning! What finesse! This
woman, my thief in the night.

This man needs a woman

Beautiful inner qualities, and ways pleasant as the oceans gentle breezes, upon my mind, soul and body her presence rests, anxieties eases.

When in need of encouragement in unsure mornings and facing day's end, femininity is waiting there for him to reassure and relax, elevating depressed hearts, demystifying blurred dreams and goals, that's the facts.

A woman's power to refocus is bar none, the touch and life presence stopping one from drowning when the will is lost to swim, a cheerleader is what this man wants, yes, this is why this man needs a woman.

# ACT II

## Crumbling Walls

It never lies

Jealously may hide its real intent, greed its true
color, covetousness its partner may lie in wait
though hell bent.

On having its way, prideful, arrogant parading
as austere, blinded by murderous rage
unapologetic and insincere.

Who can vanquish this dark knight of human nature?
"Oh" whom its spies, its color, its nature, its actions,
never lies.

## Emotional Turmoil

How does one reconcile two opposing forces attempting to
occupy the same space? What will unite disparate thoughts that
gives any soul the runs and make the aching conscience race?

With perturbing vaults that dance past logic with impunity, all
the while my emerging inner worlds seeking justifiable
congruity.

Raging torrents of emotion churning and burning thru
everybody cavity, an unwarranted roller coaster ride accented
by the force of gravity.

Where to find solid ground of emotive stability amid the
quixotic quick sand of intense feeling, its affections given to
another unreciprocated can send one reeling.

Its wanting something in one category yet really needing something else you cannot identify, so obviated, though, seemingly unrelated, taking action to change present reality undesired appear too fixated.

An emotion landscape whose boundaries are never clearly delineated, causing over growth of insecurity unabated, proliferating weeds of distrust that choke out inner peace, leaving the strongest nerves grated.

Such mental anguish and spiritual unbalance slated, one cannot really help themselves and therefore others around you feel unappreciated.

How to help oneself in this insidious script of a true Shakespearean tragedy, for if certain mental states can be labeled a disease then this in some way is a crippling malady.

Fortunately for those of us who do not want to drown in this violent sea of supreme sadness, and be driven crazy by the pernicious onslaughts of untamed psychotic madness.

There are steps that one can take to restore order to the disorderly. And graduating levels of control when strongly implemented accordingly.

Starting simply by removing negative people and things from your life that induce undue stress, adding positive people and things to your life that God would be moved to bless.

True friends and family help you bear your burden load, in your sojourn down the rockiest parts of life's road.

That right help should be given at your greatest time of need, which gives no deference toward race, social status or creed.

Time itself is said to heal all wounds the sun hides, yet it may take a life time to heal what cannot be seen and ease the immeasurable pain and untold scarring on the insides.

All the more reason then, to stay in good health, thru consistent exercise, rest and excellent nutrition, balanced hormones will lend to problem solving aesthetician.

Hobbies playing to innate talent missing or relax more deeply like times spent fishing.

Also, if you do not have these then find and develop an unlimited spiritual power source, unmatched steadying guide to help focus the mind and heart and smooth out the wayward course.

Will you determine the space between deciding wrong or right? Black or white? Run? Or stay and fight? Thus upon your head will be poured emotional stabilities anointing oil, as your no longer are the slave, instead the mighty conqueror of emotional turmoil.

# Held stuck

Many things swirling in beclouded wanderings,
confusion and mal-content to prod further continued
ponderings.

Thus eternally juxtaposed yelp! I remain not slipping
backward, yet never advancing, please help!

It this is the part that many talk about, but forget to reach
out, then help me as I am ... stuck!

## Reason Not to Marry

The motivations of the heart that moves one to marry, don't
always face squarely the harsh reality that a serious relationship
bound by god carries.

To identify what reasons one should tie the knot, contemplate
first what marriage is and most assuredly what it is not.

Those not mature enough to realize what the blessing and
responsibilities it details, may not want to meander down these
vicarious trails.

Avoid this path if its peace that one seeks win, for peace must
come first from deep within, if it is low self esteem by marrying
one seeks then be assured to face chagrin.

Then rest assured one will find themselves soon divorced and
left in a haze of self-doubt and confusion, as only you can raise
your estimation of yourself and then your own
emotional contusions.

Run from a wedding day still high on infatuation, as alimony payments also go up with future rates of inflation to your won consternation.

Make sure that you're not in love with the idea of each other or worse in love with the idea of being in love, else affection hear today is by tomorrow taking flight upon wings of a dove, mismatched expectations don't fit like hand in glove.

Hey! What if they threaten to leave if I don't commit? Shrieks they cry of insecurity, it is much like the pressure to buy "the only" house that's right for you, hastily signing the dotted line for surety, not stopping to check the source of this love relationships purity.

"Now I know I can change them" has been said by the best, yet you can't barely even change yourself when put to the test, allow each other space to breathe time to change and forget about the rest.

Will you marry only for sex? Then count on soon being very vex, as marriage based on nothing else eventually creates child support checks.

Does one seek marriage for convenience, say, to cook good down home meals, someone who's great at finding you the best deals.

Someone who will make sure your kids will be put thru school, or only sees to your material need, that not very cool.

Then maybe its status, politics, position or power, If one marries for any of these reasons, they'll suffer needlessly in divorce courts television hour.

Surely don't tie the knot with an ideal mate who is actually a mother or father figure, snap out of it! Or at the very least, wait until emotions mature and the inner child gets bigger.

Well, now family and friends say together we look cute! If that's the only basis to wed, take up modeling instead.

Make certain not to miss any photo shoot but, but, but, someone is better than a lonely life with no one right? Many a miserable, lonely marriage would beg to differ, maybe punch out your lights!

These reason and others you'll hear of are truly scary, forewarned is forearmed so pay heed please to reasons not to marry.

# Lonely

The creeping of loneliness enter perturbed
thought, creating momentary chaos doing
only what vexing trouble best does wrought.

In the interim dwells a soul with nothing to
embrace in warm loving hands, devoid of
that which meaning and purpose
commands longed for time demands.

Desire unmet ... Now set.

Toward unrewarded future plans suddenly
and coolly has made its unwelcome presence
known, loneliness leaves, doubts racing in the
 mind, and heart beating, tearful, ravaged
*Alone.*

# An unbalanced world

Side by side exists the mega rich and the ultra
poor, as seen so often played out it's underscored,
so much so that most unconsciously ignore.

Those with less get less, those with more get more
to nauseating excess, to wonder? I digress,
perplexed why so few enjoy capitalisms plunder.

Billions are plunged into desperations pot, pressure
cooking unwilling souls in a forty-hour working slot.

Masses earning an average pittance for their bravery,
diamond tipped debts drilling social economic slavery.

Religious, political and economic propaganda moving
masses, in step with hidden agendas of a handful
promising a better life and greener grasses.

In its wake, family units moral structure tumble, peace talks
fumble, in effectual promises mumble, frustrations form
violence, destroys peace and won't be made humble.

World resources sucked dry beyond environmental salvation, ignored due in part to selfishness and greed's insatiable expectation.

Why be patient for tomorrow when you can rape the planet today? Why worry about future sorrow, live a modernistic life as one may?

The repercussions of such attitudes have yet to be unfurled, and when they do <u>All</u> will taste the bitter fruitage of a not valuing balance, equity, unity of thought and harmonious actions in an unbalanced world.

Help me?

Out on a ledge, the pedalogical,
remuneration of the scatological.

That would deem this ranting mind
far from reason and fairly lost in the
hodge podge of a soul searching stricken
ill by human limitations, What mental
hospital should I seek please? A prayer for
those praying, self honesty is a start, I can't
find my way thru the chaos of lost
motivations.

Emotional deprivations? Financial
degradations? Human it is to lose one's
way occasioned.

What is the net that I must lay down my
conscious awareness. How will I help me to
help myself? What do I adjust in free thought to bear this?
Jump? Should I? From where into why?

Help!

# Closeness to suicide

Violent explosions, imminent commotions,
deep inside that which can no longer carry
heavy emotions.

Now strain, hurt, regret, unmitigated pain.

Breeding unbounded fear, a hopelessness that
dims vision, chokes happy realities, kills
reasons that hold mere existence in
derision, skew any options fragmenting
wholeness of spirit now in serious division.

Desperate times take on despite measures, ending this
vein facade called life seems like the last and only
pleasure, the perfectly logical choice one fantastically
bitter sweet treasure.

Ahh! Fantasy plays here, no more
crushing loneliness, no more frustration, and
humiliation, time to sink this blasted boat on the straits
of seemly endless agitation.

Awaken friend to the facts of life worth living, what you
get each day is commensurate with concerted giving.

No inner voices to chide, condemn or deride, imagine a
new inner voice that confidently commends and
encourages to seek opportunities for which you will not
be denied.

Stopping short of the bullet or the blade, lucidity in an
instance brings back for but a moment inner harmony's
shade.

A realization of human nature's psychological dark side,
each individuals very closeness to the edge of suicide.

# Torn

Am I slated to be a used up container, discarded on the trash
heap of emotionally wrecked souls? Because I drive and strive
for the affections of a female divine whose affections toward
another betrothed she are unwhole.

Be he an ogre or be he Romeo over which she still has
disheartening control. Aahh! Much as one on the outside
looking into relationships window at something longed for
to the eyes but already sold, fine item to be appropriated
and needed by the heart, so, so, so much to certainly hold.

Though impure stirring intentions strong to covet what is
craved unfold, this runs on a conscience that stands plagued
truth verses tortuous and unrelenting emotive afflictions, while
yet recounting principles that are laid up steadfast inside with
deep connections, keeping unwise actions in check and in so
doing, showing respect due forward marital restrictions.

Though, I'm happy that I know what's right, glad even more so
to do right with all my might, doesn't stop or ease the pain
induced by intense impulse to be with what's in sight.

Only time changing heart conditions born, the wills mission will work out for me that who I'll be with will be right ... still ...!

# Goodbye

In a world so be darkened so ignorant, so selfish, so
loveless. I no longer want to be another source of
such internal filth getting away humanities humaneness.

Today, from this day hence forth, will become the
change; the future I seek .

Now attention, soul of mine. The following are
condemned to eternal damnation
from my being.

Limited mentality ... Get out! Only accurate
knowledge and sound principle will
reign supreme.

Low self-esteem ... Leave! You heard right! A positive
self-image based on acquired self knowledge will lead to
new vistas of self explorations and self worth.

Selfishness and Greed ... Scram! More is to be
gained by empowering others and giving of self to
make the world a better place. Who's next?

Ah! Jealousy ... Beat it! As one should be happy for the
successes and blessing others receive everyone gets to
have their turn in the sun it's the way the universe works

Low self esteem ... "see ya!" "Wouldn't want to be ya!"
Belief in one's self is now the order
of this day!

Violent ways ... Be gone! As peace is the center of
everything, peace within, peace with god, peace with
everyone revolutionary. I will be the start to that which
is a world with one less violent person, my own peace-
keeping force.

Regret ... Farewell! I don't regret your leaving! Positive
action oriented plans in the now will guarantee your
never returning in the future.

Victim mentality ... Get lost! The only perpetual victims
in this world are the people who constantly keep you
around "Oh escape goat" that keeps on giving.

Quit laying around and blaming others for what you've desire but will never attain because you take more pleasure in blaming "the man," whoever that is! I choose not to be the victim anymore, choosing instead to become the aggressor of my goals attainment and people will move out of you way.

Disrespect ... Good riddance! As respect for self-lends to respect for others.

Hate ... So long! Love with its strength, courage and wisdom now binds me to all God's creation. This allows me to see with a heart of understanding appreciating the beauty in everything and everyone near me.

Unhappiness and loneliness, Goodbye! ... Having the capacity to choose one's own destiny, I choose happiness. It is the birth right of everything living. Soon those things that promote happiness make it grow and overflow inside of you, and the world will be benefited greatly by your choice. Traits or qualities not mentioned are on notice "you're not welcomed here any more."

Get gone! And Goodbye!

# Trail of tears

Such is the gory details along this path of pain that could be, anyone's life story.

Puddles turning into streams of tears, born as 1,000 pound loads of emotional luggage not jettisoned due to unexplained contagion of irrational fears.

All washed up, so soaked to the bone that I'm stuck in crater sized pot holes of insecurity, so cold so cold that in a world of 8,000,000,000+ souls this trail of tears is still traversed by the lonely.

A dangerous trialsome path, crying I ask; when will this burning liquid salt stop pouring from the troubled oceans and rivers of my soul crowded? Filling the highways and byways of what could be a happy inner life shrouded?

A calm I hope to someday find, a different path leading to contentment owed in arrears, until then I meander listlessly along a seemingly endless, trail of tears.

## Eternally jaded

Deep regret from compromising personal principles hold
dear, weak moment though sincere,

Heart shattered from divorce once maybe twice, failed
businesses, lost loved ones in death thrice.

Life playing like a scene from Macbeth? Relationships
pursued in the sights of love gone sour? Friendships
wrecked? Cars crashed? Money lost thru ignorance
power?

Should the tragedies playing out on the stage of life
forever negatively alter future choices? Turning a deaf
ear to non appreciative voices?

Along these lines one finds that one of two paths must
be chosen, the positive path leading to untold happiness
for attempting and attaining success beholden, pushing
fear and self-imposed obstacles aside engineering past
stuck states unfrozen.
Or one can proceed down the negative path of glass

always half empty, all dreams will fail, no marriage can or will last, ever doomed to be a product of my past, better sit down 'cause this could get lengthy.

The path that is stuck to most is the one will come to fruition, M.A.D., mutually assured failure is assured if one does not jettison a diseased "we all are doomed!" mental disposition.

The ultimate test upon which our lives will be graded, is how good a job we do getting unstuck from the quagmire of sorrowful despondency that suspends its prisoners in eternally jaded.

# Our mathematically disturbed existence

As humans we stand divided by class distinctions in all cultures a common denominator multiplying human misery on all shores, making us no better than supposed lower animals walking in peace amongst themselves on all fours.

None want to be an average Joe ironically on a planet populated by billions on millions all seeking to be number one, when what needs to be enumerated is all seeking to be a unified inequality where none are equal yet none we shun, still our composite thought and word and deed is an indivisible summation.

A thought though not new and should meet with zero resistance, does not! For now a perplexing problem that must be solved for y, in z moment, this is our mathematically disturbed existence.

# Stuck in a bubble

Scenic images passing by the 3-D panorama of my life,
moving and existing, ebbing and progressing while I am
on the inside looking out are the answers to my
numbness toward reality within? Where does one
search? Where does one begin? Which dimension am I in?

Is this it? Am I to indefinitely float weightless in the
currents of time, blown about by the winds of change,
yet unable to effect personal range?

What is this, a temporary nightmare or an unending
dream? Someone pass me realities needle to prick this
trouble, this transparency to consciousness and move me
back into the realm of those fully alive. Help me!
Anyone?! Please! For I remain ... stuck.

# Divorce

It is death experienced while still living, it continues to
leech from a being already spent, broken family,
distanced friends, and bewildered workmates all while
having to live and pay rent.

A feeling of inexplicable lack of attention span, derailed
feelings, overloaded mind too full to remand.

Off track realizations no longer tolerable as emotional
space is temporarily unavailable, personable psyche now
psychologically unassailable.

A horror movie of a heart ripped open and raw, is no longer able
to bear its own emotional pain, harkening to a gory sequel of
Saw.

Certainly cannot bear the pressure of attention to
another's romantic affection, it is simply too great
a drain post marital insurrection.

The only elements needed are space, time and

objectivity in abundance to wade thru the wreckage of relations ship, to restore faith in the construct of true love's structural edifice.

To build back the ability to trust oneself, to spiritually regain courage and peace, learning from the mistakes of past outmoded emotional motifs.

Heart healed from the ripping and the burning, opening and optimistically setting the sails to new possibilities of fulfilling natural companionship yearning.

Renewed emotional events worth exploring, this time having refueled on much self knowledge and personal growth as an outpouring, becoming a stronger, better person for enduring.

Now parents and children involved together can set a new course, and sail past the emotional wreckage called divorce.

# Temptation

It's the luxury car I want but is ridiculously costly, the
double chocolate cake downed with a supersized frosty.
You just know it comes with zits, weight gain, blood
sugar problems and so much more it will cost me.

Were those STD's really worth giving in to illicit desire?
And because you abandoned your moral principles some
things on your body will stay constantly on fire.

This is the problem with anything that tempts,
selfishness and immediate gratification will hold you in
contempt.

Satisfaction now is put ahead of reason, rationality, logic
and with consideration of dire consequences suffered,
unimagined pain to be paid to the tempted for personal
imperfections proferred.

Cannot be child like in reaching out for wants that we rarely ever need yet rationalize that we can't live without, self discipline, moral strength and exercise of faith will make our resolution stout.

To conquer future enticements we must vanquish that inner itch, it comes from fighting numerous spiritual battles of restraint that make one inner rich.

Allurement is always an enemy and never of trustworthy station, stab it dead without hesitation or prepare to live a life of enslavement to long lived temptation.

# Opinion

Everyone's birthright, our preconceived filters for
interpreting our world, forming beliefs, and motivating
action, determining life's ultimate satisfaction.

If opinion is tainted, mental diarrhea ensues, whose spin
on this moment to moment existence in the panorama of
reality we call life has more substantive constitution? Is
one's opinion made more relevant if it solves problems
or raises issues of social conscience that have no easy
solution?

Rulers make rules based on it, shaping and framing
public opinion made policy, business leaders pontificate
with it, saying their superior and buying into it will help
calm societal ills and realign the planetary oddity.

Religious leaders insist theirs is backed by divine
approval as guide for our lives as a perennial equinox,
And any opinion other than theirs is heretically
unorthodox.
The problem with said opinions is when no truth exists

outside of what they say truth is especially when its
construct seems hollow, when any one buys into any
process, way of thinking or action without thought or
question, then it is propaganda when other opinions are
forbidden then human rights violations are sure to
follow.

Opinions as a matter of course are not rules, not a code
of conduct and not necessarily truthful causality, what is
scary is when its accuracy is not on the same plane as
reality.

It may be just imagination, a way of thinking things
through, thus the onus is on the bearer to prove opinion
and assumption as gospel too.

Whatever each one determines it to be, it is just being
itself, an opinion, nothing more and nothing less that's
why its free.

# Tired

A world of somnambulists never fully awake but not
quite asleep, scurrying down life's highways and
byways but barely at a creep.

Same mental state in the worrisome days as well as in
the more worrisome nights, bills piling up higher than
dirty dishes, chores never fully completed as one wishes.

Family priorities being displaced by low priority to
mundane doing, caught on the treadmill running a rat
race and never get the cheese for all that pursuing.

Why are we running this rat race? I don't particular care
that much for cheese as I'm lactose intolerant, I need rest
and less stress! That is it, a warm and abiding pace.
Woman's tempers short and flaring, no time to rest and
too tired for child rearing.

No time for mate, no time of self, way too wired! So
many needs to fill, are they really needs? Whoever is at
the helm of this life needs to get fired!! (No wait,
that's me?!)

Tired of terrorism and violence, where do people get the
energy for this stupid stuff? Tired of economic
uncertainty and unrest, enough is enough.

Too tired for mudded issues, too rushed to stop and pay
attention, too fatigued to think, I know it sounds bad but
too tired to care or even garner inappropriate
apprehension.

Anxieties of life extinguishing spirituality, someday
hope to get back on track, big goals and big dreams and
business schemes, yeah, that old tack.

Oh well, right now I'm too tired to eat and too hungry to
sleep, just sitting here stuck in the existence of being,
staying, remaining always tired.

# Hypocrisy's mask

Hiding in the darkness of human intent is an identity dodging, fleeing from truth, devoid of self knowledge and entrapped by ignorance. No self worth, no self esteem, no honoring others since to thine own self it remains untrue as happenstance.

It should be exhausted as it forever dons pretenses, that veil the souls bedarkened character as whitewashed fences.

Even in its death it anonymously stays true to task, seeking the cover of conventional morality to remain hypocrisy's mask.

# Irrationality of fear

Standing on the precipice that is your life facing an
ocean below if infinite possibility is fear, a mental
handicap, an emotional disability creating obstacles
that successfully entrap.

An unreasoning self induced psychosis fashioning
reality out of fantasy, a potentially life threatening
disease tying up vast inner resources in pompous
formality.

Impractically efficient it is in ignoring facts, betraying
truth and insulting logic for spite, chooses not to see
justice and holiness in all that is good and right.

Prejudges before examining facts, running like a child
from delusional alarms only it can hear, sounds alarms
of anxiety over threats that are just not there.

Prudish in its presumptuous nature, crops up only when

doubt or worry shakes us, unprincipled in it successful
nomenclature and spoken eloquently when racism
prejudice wakes up.

Other people's negative opinions and unchecked
emotions can foment lynch mobs, prayer and
steadfastness to correct principles can counter what
irrational fear robs.

Sobriety stocks the fires of right standards and to
positive thinking appeal, indeed, these can help us
conquer false evidence appearing real.

Confidently step into oceans of possibilities and once
their, completely destroy this irrationality of fear.

# ACT III

## Rising from the Ashes

## Positive Thinking

Positivity taken to pleasantly contrived places
moves the heart to desire what boundaries the
mind traces thru inventive and perceptive.

Inner co-mingling the power to change one destiny
sounded aloud in its ringing. Shattering antiquated
beliefs while embracing enlightened paradigms.
Continuously seeking new and accurate knowledge
in good times and bad times.

What the future holds is what the past warned of and
the minds present agenda has slated so that what is yet
experienced happens not by chance no, but by force
thought. It's created imagination and innovation
capsulated in consistency deliberately revamping
itself.

Ascending upon wings of its own expanding propensity,
vicariously holding its course unmovable with dogged
pertinacity.

A wonderfully good attitude is positivity's rule not its exception, the principle ingredient in greatness since times inception.

So if one previously had no clue, awareness, grasp or inkling, then it's time to embrace the charisma, the charm and generative nature of positive thinking.

# The Spice of life

Jasmine and ginger added make the
so ... so ... and hum drum ... yum yum,
kinswoman and brown sugar make the
dead living.

Salt and pepper changes bland to a tasteful
misgiving. Please accept my mint and dill
transforming hot temperament to cool when
calm is needed, her garlic and parsley make
the most hated dish life serves up, easier to
digest when heeded.

One needs a good spice one needs a good wife.
She is never late but always on thyme, her
cinnamon, her spice affects deeply ... the
spice of life.

# Acted Upon Dream Come True

When wishes are born and reported in the
conscious mind contrite, this is where the
thought and intention unite.

That move the idea and the deed to take flight,
rise above the troubles of the day as
the carefree clouds and stars of the night
so bright.

If one's delight is to work hard consistently and
smartly to attain the goals, position with successful
planning then what is substance will take form when
proper supervision enrolls.

Ah! Then for surety what is envisioned
is what will shape itself to the characteristics
you imbue, then and only then do acted upon
dreams come true.

## My Handyman

How do I love thee? Let thee count the sprays of
paint interior and exterior. Except on rainy days
blessed are mistaken, base boards as they will be
laid at no added cost.

Blessed are those subcontractors that showed for
work since the rest most certainly got lost, "I know
the carpenter"! So many others claim, my handy
man though, knows tons of them and can outbid them
all on quality and cost and pick the best ones out by name.

That Tom he's the man with the plan!

I'm not kidding! Seriously!
He's got the whole blueprint in his hand,
He's got the blueprint in his hand. (end chorus)

If this house a double fudge layer cake, then you'd
definitely put your foot in it! We thank you profusely,
for your generous concrete outpouring. Helping us
deposit cheaper carpet for now than expensive
hardwood flooring.

But for the grace of sod plan were grateful to have
had a building experience like we had planned,
Thanks in part to my trusty handyman!

How do you know its true love?

When you know their short comings,
personality, flaws and strength, when
you can account for all their
emotional baggage and can list them
at length.

When you're aware of all these things
about them and accept it anyway,
When you still want to wake up by that
person's side for eternity and a day.

When you know enough about yourself
to know that your life will never be the
same without them, this special one
never again to be without sweet
thoughts of love, individual
peculiarities fit together like hand
in glove.

When two see eye to eye financially,
spiritually and with good chemistry, grow
together in emotional intimacy, then, that is the
way it ought to be.

With energy like two worker bees, thought
and word and deed combine and tail dove, together
in a whisper three little words ... it's true love.

## Poor Background

It is said that you can't take the person out of the neighborhood, but can take the neighborhood out of the person, this may only be true if the individual has internalized only the bad experiences 'Wrapping the soul and causing innate virtues to worsen.

Creating an entity whose life perspective is devoid of spiritual vision, robbed of dignity characterized.

By violated conscience that spew more negativity into a world already morally devastated, when negativity is thus returned in kind sadly bad attitudes are hardened and validated.

In exponentially heightened form concentrated, and in so doing self limiting boundaries are imposed creating impoverished thoughts perpetuated. With crushing poverty resulting in diminished spheres of perceived opportunity demonstrated.

I don't believe this downward spiraling vortex of victim mentality has to hold anyone prisoner of their past at all.

Instead I choose to believe that everyone can reunite and override poor thoughts and feelings of negativity, replacing them with healthy and virtuous principles of positivity.

Standing proud, standing tall, moving the spirit onward, the soul now moving the mind toward worthwhile goals and thoughts generating new priorities ever up-lifted.

Opportunities become unlimited as new vistas now reached for seem attainable, new perspectives on the world that changing old paradigms waxing rearrange able, soft pliable more trainable.

Many might disagree with this mental gyration stated, yet this process of change plays itself out in everyone who has and who is now inspiring toward greater stature slated.

For these ones wealth and recognition will overtake them, if they refuse to remain a slave to the past and won't back down, then and only then will everybody move from stigma, breaking the chains heal the pains no longer manifest in coming from a poor background.

# The dance of life

Life in many ways is a dance personified. Due in part to each person listening to their minds, goals, hearts being attuned to using the dictates as a guide. One can learn love's dance with others in good fun and harmony or Waltz with that special someone in synch with each other on key coordination, relationships in movement of a 100 piece symphony.

Hey, life should be fun, fast and furious as Quickstep, lighthearted as East Coast Wing or slow and groovy as each can do life's own thing. Passion's flames heat up in intensity as sexuality expressed in the slow fore play of a Bolero, a soft sexy Rumba manifest moving intimate, closeness of dancers. A Tango merging two people heart to heart at desires crest.

When it is time for a break from life's affair, time to take long strides thru the park engaged in a Fox Trot without care. So what if onlookers stare, they only wish they could have as much fun dancing thru life, but to chase after real happiness they wouldn't dare. That's for sure is crazy! For while living might as well strive to be alive.

Hey, wanna Jive? or how about a Salsa Merengue with lots of hip motion? Oh yeah! Throw yourself into whatever you love exceeding until body and mind get the notion of successes uniquely formulated potion.

Yes, dance is generative and needed, definitive and seeded with humanity's great innate desire exuded, to attain universal harmony oneness extruded.

To fully understand why we're created in such a way will take intensive introspection under the scalpel of eternity's knife. Till such time arrives you'll find me happily engaged in a Pasa Doble or Samba rife, with the elegance and power timed in steps putting together .... the dance of life.

# The world is not all black and white

Help me please to comprehend the stereo typical fallacies of ignorance's pervasiveness. Whom it comes to unwarranted beliefs about prejudices held unconsciously feeding racisms dogged abrasiveness.

In a country that prides itself on tolerance and information superhighways enlightenment. Yet unwritten agenda's are still scrolled on people's hearts and minds fastening mistrust and fomenting deep seated resentment.

In dispelling old myths I will be the first to berate antiquated views seeing how one deals squarely with reality so late, now let's set the record straight.

Should there be white Justice? And black justice? In some cases unfortunately "yes." But knowing one's rights and doing what's right can make justice to be administered fairly if only under duress.

Is there white money or black money? It should only be green. Is there white poverty and black poverty? No! That both will be treated with societal disdain is diseased and plainly seen.

Is their white knowledge and black knowledge? No! Only accurate knowledge that helps one become determined to separate truth from hear say.

Is there black death and white death? No! Since only red blood runs from all those victimized and mourning to pray.

Are there black people and white people? No! In reality, they are only two out of many, variations on the genetic theme of humanity. Whether there is a black or white child born both should have the same rights and privileges or society. As such there are no black dreams and white dreams only realistic goals and plans worked upon with sobriety. So that what is strived for is honesty achieved with successful notoriety.

Is there such a thing as speaking black? Or speaking white in terms of good communication? Or shouldn't all empower themselves with knowledge and embrace intelligence instead of ignorance and stupidity dictating one's station.

Are there black foods and white foods? No! Only nutritious food that should be eaten by all races and culture of society. That can encourage good health if one advances themselves to wholesomeness in sumptuous variety.

For one to continue to think in black and white in a world of color richly woven in its tapestry is to ignore the majestic forest of life for only seeing a few pathetic trees. When the reality of truth is not as we want it, but as it is, then the lamp of the soul will burn bright.

The sooner that we acknowledge and accept that the world in not all black and white then we will all be in living color.

# Who is "The Man"?

Who is "the man" that black folks talk about? Is it a white man in a suit in a dark upper room carrying clout? Weaving mischief to suppress black men by blocking opportunity and soul searching literacy? Removing self identity while concocting multifaceted and far reaching, politically incorrect and culpable conspiracies?

If true, he should be placed on America's most wanted list, if by plausible theoretical argument he does exist. However, I think this man that many seek has no physical form or personal identity. No, but instead exists inside us all, wait a minute you say, how could this be?

"The Man" is preconceived notions of how things should be? Intellectually, emotionally, morally and sexually. It filters out color because it thinks too many colors aren't right. So he builds a dreary dream world that's only black and white. What it loves, it loves despite being psychologically ill, and what it hates it will just as easily kill.

Thus, the man is none other than prejudice, jealously, hate, envy and greed, it's humanities dark side that is engendered in this ugly breed.

"The man" will sink to lowest lows and hang high and dry, will beat you black and blue cause what is its target must die. You can't lock up bad qualities or arrest what you can't touch and feel, those who give him life must be educated that his existence is not real.

If he's not empowered then he'll have no influence at all, his power will be scanty and nations can rejoice at what he'll be fall. So remove him from your mind and heart greatly reducing strife, then a rich new inner world will lead you to a prosperous new outer life. In effect, you'll lock "The Man" up and throw away the key, the day you determine he'll not exist or gain leverage inside of you and me.

## Cathartic Thought

Tracings drawn by impression and
thoughts pacing, impassioned erratic
pleas racing.

Thru the quandary of unsolicited ills, ever
flowing frothy and agitated turning light to
blackness and chills.

Decisive reform, the only curve for hesitancy's
imperfection, emotional constipation, hope
softening consternation.

An open mind, the fiber of cemented thinking, and a
bloated stomach of inflexible views shrinking. Phew!
I'll make my fluid thoughts salient and bright and my
nourishing contemplations light.

# Good Things Come to Those Who Wait

My life once a complex conundrum, boring
and humdrum, awakened to the flavor of love
with the taste of Jamaican rum.

She, the beauty, adjoining me, and kindness so
sweet, companionship danced and romanced now
conjoined replete.

The trappings of love's trueness attained, now
loneliness the prisoner is over due to be
arraigned, following the leadings of conscience
properly trained.

Patience rewarded, instant
gratification retarded.

Just as good eating results from a slow cooked,
well prepared plate, so does the mind and heart
feel satisfaction when it is primed and ready for a
truly committed relationship, the great reward for
those who wait.

# The scenery of my life

Gladsome attitudes unpretentious platitudes paint
my skies blue, imaginations set free and wild give
feather light clouds in my eyes a jovial white hue.

Love embodies the roots and strengthens the trunk
of my trees, providing fruits of kindness divorced
from anxieties.

Truth given freely, caressed and cleansed gently by
generosities breezes, settling mind and soul at eases.

Shades of peace, grass so soft and green, faith soaring
as birds carefree and serene.

Conscience and conscientiousness budding pride and
confidence strutting, bright futures flower of fragrant
flair flooding.

Heralding, endless variety and humanness, what shouldn't we be willing to do, attaining to higher purpose to maintain this?

Beauty and intimacy allowed to grow wild and rife, with inner expressions that color the scenery that is my life.

# A positive view

Sensational, inspirational is the feeling
experienced in the moment as an old day
ends and a new day is spawned. Bringing
opportunities which ends to trends, which
love nurtures and wisdom attends.

In a way, in a word in a song never heard,
wrong desire deferred, impure thought deterred.

Soulful in the intangible, employed dutifully in
expressed principle.

Life streams along properly addressed, positivity
of feeling solely manifest.

Emitted rapaciously from a centered inner being,
who grow and grows without end no limits to
greater seeing.


Widening out in accord with limitless belief,

thereby mentoring virtue, destroying in the
process, limitations maddening grief.

Hence, the possible and probable coexist and
ascend elevated anew ever expanding and
increasing in a positive view.

# Human Potential

I alone explorer of emblazoned voracity, uniquely decided upon
entering the realms that envelope the depth and breadth of
human capacity.

A universe barely scratched by the totality of current scientific
pondering, the more one finds out the more one
keeps wondering.

As what humans have grasped thus far is mere simplistic
blundering, with such humbling realizations and
disheartening refrain.

I redouble my efforts to journey once again my thoughts a
perpetual machine driven with the engine of an imaginative
curious mind. Explore all limitless possibilities that can be
conjured in kind.

In order to arrive at the inner sanctum of generated ideas
centered, depends fully upon the positive degree of detailed
past input, future applied, presently entered.

Off the perpetual motion machine runneth the interplay of reality and rhapsody in an instant of rhyme, reaching never seen landscapes an enigma in time.

What makes the minds of boundless curiosity? And fascination is due to its dynamic propensity to evolve and involve without the slightest hesitation.

Absorbing new knowledge, recreating, rewriting its own script, thereby expanding its own ability to do what it does ever more well equipped.

It can manufacture new branches of 10,000 lane highways, re-engineer around new obstacles successfully meandering the challenges of life's byways.

As long as no self-limiting beliefs are placed upon it, then it can be free to manufacture idea's that run the gauntlet quantified, of magnificent visions emboldened to greatness affording changes in synaptic connections recording dignity qualified.

By exercise of intellect and consciences justified an idea machine utilizing the body as its idealistic extension, efficiently and effectively, accomplishing planned goals devoid of apprehension.

What master plan such a highly ordered organism will play out, no doubt quintessential, exploring our peerless inner universe and unleashing the fullest expression of our human potential.

# Not another pretty face unknown

Amassing road blocks of imagined intellectual
excuses, negative types playing self sabotage,
inflicting self abuses.

"O that I coulda ," then maybe "I shoulda"
possibly even "I woulda."

Displayed aggression producing a more
assertive tone, avoiding the crime of being serial
failure prone, vowing from this day hence forward
that not another pretty face is unaccomplished and
unknown.

Terrorism's end

On wings of eagles sighted, hence
truth be heightened, feelings to anger
whence due in-sighted.

Desired in the soul is how can
freedom from it ring, why terrorism is
the form and nature of its sting.

For it robs all of peace of mind, foments
war's sentiments to be returned in kind.

Tragedy that results from loss of
innocent life, cuts deeper than the
physical stabbings and spiteful twisting
of a depraved man's knife.

In the wake of cowardly acts the
chards of crying and weeping,
spiritual healing is what its victims
are always seeking, looking for hope,
for comfort, and answers realistically
speaking.

Blood spilled, vengeful outcries for
peace to be enacted, jurisprudence
thoroughly exacted, anti-terrorist
protocols initiated to halt and contain
those with evil intent ever more
impacted.

Yet, is it possible to remove hatred
from hate filled hearts by peace
keeping forces or judiciary congress?
or instead will it only put on the alert
such one's who may or may not yield
or confess? Even under the most
violent duress?

What then will it take to remove all
violence and hatred by which
endeavors of men thus far are at best
inferior? Circumstance then could
only change by the action plan and
will of one who by nature in all ways
is far superior.

One who is never taken by surprise,
searches all hearts with his own
beaming eye, hears the sincere one's
plaintiff cries.

Only the haughty and wicked prayers
does He despise, due to impure
thoughts and lies, proceeding in
darkness of unwholesome ways
unwise, against such things a Being
of love decries.

When He comes to judge by one
standard all mankind will be his
captor, forever gone will be those
who loved the monstrosities of
violence in mankind's sickest
chapter.

When all the wrongs will have been
righted, the savage brutality of

twisted men short sighted,
beautifully correct and humane ways
no longer blighted.

Peace will then prevail because it
will be what each right hearted one
wants, no racist taint, no ugly
religious paint, no divisive immoral
ideologies and nationalistic taunts.

No, instead all must learn and
conform to a humble divine agenda
constituted to the language of peace,
instructed in scripture, inspired of the universal
sovereign, magnified by Christ, glorified by a life of truth
lived applied impartially for eternal release.

A war is to be waged and this is for
sure, though not with rhetoric, knifes,
guns or mines, this war is to be fought
spiritually on the frontiers of the heart,
soul and minds decidedly acts to choose
ways never cruel only kind.

The erasure of propaganda shaping
motive and hidden agenda's giving
motivation, truth twisted to evil
notion, sending ripples of negative
energy in seismic waves thru justice's
agitated ocean.

Terrorism old and jaded must and
will end soon, history reported
reveals it, divine prophecies seals it,
a bright future of multifaceted
peaceful humans swoon.

Soon all wrongs are to be corrected, all
violence will be deflected, when educated
love is fostered by all justice will be reflected.

To enjoy such a bright future all must
change now and ascend, the mountain,
the elevation of man's hastening to a new
beginning with terrorism end.

I need more time!

How does one need more of something
he or she can't fully grasp, yet explain?
Without enough of it there is no balance,
too much stress, no happiness to gain.

This commodity is unseen but makes
itself known. It is intangible yet it shortage
can be felt, to the great and to the small it
is equally dealt.

The prince fully utilizes it and the pauper
wastes it all, it is by it we attain success
and how fortunes rise and fall.

It cannot be weighed, yet all
of us feel its rock, not measured on scales
but by the ticking of the clock. It's
priceless really, it's passing judges our
values, sizes up our goals and causes those
aware of how precious each moment's
passing is to take stock.
Oh that I could quantify it, package it, and mass

produce it cheaply. Then reality of time would play on my terms sublime, I could save it for a rainy day, no one ever making the excuse of not having enough time.

When peace will permanently prevail

A healing from emotional turmoil quelled,
freedom from guilty conscience torments
dispelled.

Escape from wicked racist intent
threatening personnel harm, release from
economic pressure that signals survivals
alarm, abandonment of political and religious
notions that have long ago lost their charm.

Higher divine principles to which
all conform, creating conditions that
make one and all feel safe and warm.

When light and truth and peace are what all
seek themselves to avail, one universal
definition of sovereignty the masses assail,
then and only then, is when true peace will
permanently prevail.

# A nonchalant summer day

One warm sunny day, heads swaying
to the dictates of the radios beat.

Fingers now snapping, in tune to
feet tapping.

While at ease gliding down the traffic
lanes of life's time, engine racing with
hearts pacing in synch with this happy
rhyme.

What we'll accomplish or not is entirely
arbitrary, hope nothing is very serious
about anyone destination, no quite to
the contrary.

We're taking it easy today, no worries
man! No trepidation, we won't have any
problems, only situations.

Just saying "hi", and waving to strangers walking
to me, exchanging light banter as socialite buzzing
of bees.

Lazily ambulating down the ubiquitous path that is
life's lane, with the clouds dancing still
as clouds do best, sending free showers of rain.

Making light of each other's carefree plight, ill emotions
held at bay, there in the nonchalant ramblings of a
typical summer's day.

# Tact

I realize now that I need to definitely be
more discrete about who I tell what about,
when, how and why's, I don't have to dodge
questions or tell straight out lies.

Just tell them the least that needs to be said,
move onto new topics and subjects just read.

If subject to a tirade of piercing interrogation,
don't capitulate on your stand or give in by
abrogation.

Whether factual or strong opinion tracking,
diplomacy is tact in fancy packing.

Your views expressed and sincerely accepted as a well-timed gift
or wedding ring. World leaders skillfully use it, no one can ever
abuse it.

Keep it in mind when you want all your

words to impact, It will serve you well, thus never
dispel the greatness, the principle that is ... *Tact.*

## Moving on

Trying in earnest to bypass the memories etched in the middle of the mind, strong feelings and desire deeply anchored in the soul in ways that seem unkind.

Emotions carved into a heart calloused over from grieving for a past bereft of future win, of what could and would and should have been.

It is immoral, a punishable sin to cast into the dungeon of intimate relationship bygone, psychological tortures from here to Saigon.

My present feeling no longer guarantees payment of future emotional rewards still missed, the hurt inside is replayed constantly like a sadist wish.

In its infernal madness why o please God make it end, I've had enough so so weary, I think it's time to make things mend.

Let time heal the wounds inflicted and carry the hard lessons learned, moving forward one step and each day one step stronger earned.

Periods of relief from grief getting longer so that may ...

# Enough said

Some books touted are better left unread

Some thoughts stated are better left unsaid

Some men of ill will exalted are better left for dead

Some goals pursued are better left abandoned for

higher ideals instead and if one taken aback understands

the reasons for the aforementioned stated, then enough said.

# The gravity of words

The pen may be mightier than the sword, but the words that the pen give birth to are of a more powerful accord.

Words can move millions by sheer weight of profoundness, cause tanks to stand still by linguistic uniformity of logical soundness.

Shaking rigid thoughts and inflexible paradigms from its rusted foundations, foments changes and decidedly rearranges whole nations.

The constitutional destinies of untold generations lifts discouraged spirits and sends imaginations soaring, ever seeking to explore inner worlds and planets of humanities creative and expressive outpouring.

One syllable of negativity can send waves of social ineptitude across oceans of positivity, so much so that linguistic axes perpetuate a preponderance of proclivities.

Therefore, be most careful that what we speak and write

eventually affords, a great depth and breadth of force that can now be felt in the gravitational movement of words.

# Creativity

The hands of creativity print master strokes of words upon the canvas of man's restless mind, listless by extension the soul moving from one degree of imagination to the next in search of something greater than itself to define.

Possibly to merge created it to do what one does, if only just because.

Thus furthering still greater creativity and fueling more imaginative thoughts that will never ever end as the end is a beginning in itself.

# Formula 500 mind

One million horse powered neurons kicking out hot,
vivacious ideas calmed by confident oxygen super cooled,
and turbo charged supportive glucose fueled.

Never acts until it checks its systems twice, motivated by
passion throttling unlimited innovation concise.

Imaginative yearning leaving a legacy of achieved dreams,
burning tracks in the synaptic grid of hybrid schemes.

In the case of parents inspiring high octane goals, open
wheeled domination leaving room to choose where
achievement rolls.

Everyone can win at this race of life determination spinning,
formulaic effort till one reaches the circle of winning.

Revved up action applies power of the focused kind, and puts
the pedal to the medal of a formula 500 mind.

## Booklover

The passion of words ringing in concentric patterns of a kind,
that reveals love of language that one does not often find.

Words penned is a life march ideally composed of imagination
expressive in its transition, murderous intent and blind
ambition.

Love mystically written in the heart is demystified in the
movement of pen to page, firing bombs of emotive rage.

Unifying mind and soul mounted on linguistic steeds, that
brings out the best and the worst of each human's character
defined by the subjects a person reads.

The heat of inner battles intensifying causing intellect to run
for book covers, knowing that victories of will and goals noble
will be attained by all booklovers.

## Stages of satisfaction

The tricking of compassion dripping from aching hearts,
beating and overflowing, a longing from all their parts.

Owning companionship and sparkling soul stirring emotional
and electrical energies, hotly charged transforming elating
thoughts and idealisms, fantasy to chemical and emotional
realities.

Free of trouble and dismay, for all the world to see on
continual display.

Muted goals and desires performing charismatic somersaults,
fueling the visions of power plants as it ought.

Lighting brightly the stage of real life action, real love, real
happiness, lights ..., cameras ..., satisfaction!!

## Uncaged thoughts

Creativity, seen roaming freely through open fields of ideas, basking in the light of freedom of expression, affected by the spring breezes of quiet contemplation.

Imagination galloping wild along the boundless tundra of endless possibilities, howling at the moon in wild fights with self limiting dreams, feeding night time hostilities.

Seeking food for thought and forever chasing the clouds of tomorrow's rising potential, human thinking and reasoning need to be disciplined, restrained and domesticated if it is to be providential.

Some thoughts, however, are always better off left uncaged.

# A new life shared

A new life created from inward parts, the generative powers of two unified hearts.

From this moment forward two lives forever changes, crazy thoughts and old notions of life probability baby completely rearranges.

New thoughts fashioned by large doses of reality, two minds racing with provocative possibility.

Boundless love of mother and father will help ground this young life in proper psychosocial imprinting, shield it from the miscarriages of immoral expediency sprinting.

The maturity of Godly wisdom will form strong its frail and tender constitution, nurture it to exercise mountain like faith of hallelujah resolution.

Hence, no amount of money, time and energy is to be spared, in guiding, educating, and directing the course now initiated by a new life shared.

# Sweet songs

The radio clicks on serving plates of choice tunes well arranged, for fingers N Synch to tasty sounds pleasingly exchanged.

The music lover's palate widely ranging, effecting tones of prune like regularity, compositions dishing distortions to satiate the acoustic appetite from the classical to the funkadelic.

Melodious varieties meet with satisfaction playing out in flavorful and obsequious throngs, as it longs for the dainty, ethereal appeal of the sweetest songs.

# Tenacity

A vision seen clearly, a desire pursued clearly, a concept by
persistence held steadfastly.

That time once conceived to be of worth is to be attained
worthily in dignified manner, is to die for if it is to be had at all
under the symbol of pertinacity's banner.

Boldness will tell a story of grand repose in the life of any
that overcome adversity, valiance advances forth to claim its
diploma from the school of hard knocks university.

The sacrifice, the blood and sweat that is the strong suit of
such voracity, never giving up or giving in is the very essence of
tenacity.

# ACT IV

## Wisdom's Growth

# Life seasons

In the spring of life's freshness masks discouragement,
with each cloud seeks, appreciating one's prime snow
capped peaks.

Racing hormones and sun kissed mountain ranges.
Set in non sweltering heat of life's summer goals,
ongoing anticipated challenges created, adjusting to
now adult roles.

Unrealized, fall arrives evoking midlife reflection on
chosen and un-chosen paths taken, wishes and youthful
desires forsaken, trusting relationships forged as well as
shared, confidence shaken.

Winter's precarious etching color, some gray majestic
and dignified, whole others old beaten, decrepit mortified.
That time has passed and was not wisely spent, now little
can be done to change this cold reality now with arthritic
joints and back bent.

Some to exult in legacies, they've forged from which the next generation will have its spring, sadly some will seek solace in ending their regret and hopelessness with suicides string.

One can choose how the phases of one's experiences will begin and end as opportunities remain rife, to create how one wants to have the fullest of each season that is life.

Exorcise your apparitions

Each of us is born plagued by the shadows of the
imperfect human condition, discerned with time
and to temperance expanding intuition.

An ethereal sixth sense fishing out imagined frights,
a haunting of bedarkened days rudely bestirring
sleepless nights.

Accurate knowledge of universally divine things
brightened, the void of ignorance, tempestuously
vilifying thoughts soul enlightened, domains of false
reason unreality erase hope, contort vision rob all of
inner riches.

Careful lest the future be permanently blighted, look to
stars of unfettered dreams sighted.

Stretch and grow where inner ghosts can't taunt you.

Become expansive in thought, a giant among reason.
Grow in confidence as now is the time to exorcise
your self-imposed demons.

# Quality

All companies desire it, employees who
lack it? They fire it! Anything that represents
it? They' hire it, marriages improved by it,
customer's demand it. Both rich and poor alike
will pay top dollar for it!

Yet this concept it can be almost anything to
anyone at any given time. A process?
An enigma? A riddle? What fiddles the riddle?
A fiddle made better by a seasoned fiddler
exhibits it unawares.

An inner drive perhaps? That seeks to crack
the code in newly discovered genetic base pairs.
It listens? To new sounds, its sees the world thru
new eyes. A feeling? Innately manifested in a job
well done. A thought? Unasked for before even
begun. An intangible principle? Never fully qualified
by anyone yet once fully expressed is recognized
unerringly by everyone. A means to an end?
An end that justifies its means?

An end of its own accord? A fixture? In the fabric
of holding together the universe, governing the
physical realm of sentient beings summarizing
anything that humans desire and envision, always
present everywhere and nowhere.

This of course is a quality exercise that has just been
engaged in. Hum? While I'm to make sure you live
a quality life before its quality is lost, never mind
that you can't hold quality.
Just grab as much as you can?!!!

## Ode to Summer Morning

A haunting mist drenching summer dreams kissed by the graces
of dew, now recognized in the day once playing stranger to
bleach blotted black velvet imaginings
of night about to turn blue.

What will your touch do?

Will it spark in others clear and keen insight?
Will it help young ones walk sure footed with
dignity light? Will it transmit hope of future days beaming
rainbows made to shine more bright?

Will it inspire dreams of greater servitude than
selfish fights over rights?
Such is your power ... Unleash it!!

Glass collection of blunders

The promises that we didn't keep,
Frozen in stained glass relief
Regret, disdain, embittered belief
Bygone reminders painfully collected
Entombed in wooden resentment deflected
Inventoried "Oh my!" and amassed "What have I
done?!"

A word of friendly advice, don't hold on to such
a twisted collection.

Speak for your
forefathers

As a living testimony of their past failures that
your future can now make success anew.

Listen to their voices each day as history speaks
thus of their noble bearing pure and true,

Be the embodiment of gene pool thoughts still
echoing thru time to fill their right place in you,

Your words will sharpen, your deeds will harken
to all the voices of your forefathers.

Thanks
for
bringing
me
up today


Lifting my spirits given wings of eagled flight,
restoring winds at hope that uplift future's bright,
imagination soaring thru clouds creative soaked
in the light.

I'll remain sky bound from this rebound.

Do you hear the oceans of
my life?

Waves spontaneity crash on the shores of day to
day realities, must become like water in dealing
with such formalities.

The ingress of advantages shimmer, the egress of
lost moments glimmer.

You have been there for each wave inevitably
thrashing, the joys and pains brought with each
crashing.

Most grateful you've paid attention to
each wave.

Dust off the dreams:


that have laid rusting dormant in the basement
of inspiration, gathering cobwebs born
of timidity and reservation.

Spiders will get mad at your new found
movements stagger, disturbed at awakened
dreams transformed to goals achieved
with swagger.

If the dust mop of my gentle prodding is enough
to make you prove, then 1'll do more regular
dusting to keep your dreams on the move.

Make sure you

       march with time


Can't beat it, escape it or make it, Only match your
steps to its consistent cadence to join up with it.

No wayward moments, no off track kilter,
Fabulous riches or stark poverty defined in the
sway of your use of time filter.

Love it or hate it, pay attention! For we all have it
the same, and when the march ends there
is no one to blame.

Continue making the most of your march

I tweeded

you the other day:


Because, long ago, I gotten woven in your silky
way, dacron of desire was on display.

We encountered unplanned rips and too many
tears, all stitched up just in time to
allay mismatched fears.

Seeking a rayon of hope spun for longer days
crocheting you and I together, our unique tapestry of love
interweaving the texture of our life lived into pure leather.

I

Seeded

you

when

you weren't looking

Planted you in the soul of benefit without a doubt,
exposed you to the sun's rays of lighted knowledge
to help creative seed sprout.

Fertilized you with confident conviction,
uprooted surrounding weeds of doubt and
cumbersome restriction.

Now, go make the world a benefactor of your
fully ripened power fielded, make sure to share
freely all the good fruits yielded.

Put a little
moo in it


Keep grazing the worlds field of life's many
choices, listen to the tall grass of many voices.

Chew them over wisely, let others taste and
test besides thee.

Let it ferment still from the doubled stomached
vault of discernment pull, milk each opportunity
for its worth full.

Keep mulling over important matters then keep
mooving right along.

Are you the super dad of legendary fame?

Who sees through poor excuses, raising
standards all things being the same?

A tower of integrity? Leaps tall homework
assignments stalwart, yet gritty?

Known for larger than life problem solving
feats in his city?

He's a dee-aye-dee-dee-y complete, a legendary
super parental titan that stands
replete!

Sure is a lot of
mama drama lately


Stimulate young academic minds to reach out for
greatness, tidy up those rooms as we'll not debate this,
respect and etiquette along with strict rules about
lateness.

Eat up those veggies as strong bodies is what you extol, you
deserve an Emmy for best daytime drama in a child rearing role,
these primetime leading ladies who should truly be awarded for
stories that rarely get told.

Thermo
nuclear
kindness-ism's
detonating


Weapons of atomic mass comfort strewn upon landscapes of
Joyful thanksgiving, expanding in concentric circles of taking
and giving.

Leaving charred restraints of peaceful restitution upon
the ground zero of brotherly love.

A battle worth fighting for on plain of life's fieldings, thank you
for your many ground-to-air explosive kindnesses yielding.

## The REAL loser

Is the one losing himself trying to win at all cost?
Not learning from mistakes means learning
opportunities are lost.

Don't see making errors as stepping stones to success, sore
losers don't want to face the bare truth under stress.

The real winners manage well the fallout between their ears,
formulate new strategies, gain new self knowledge and conquer
their fears.

I love the way winners lose!

How's the
Psychological
Traffic?


Driven crazy lately yet still demonstrating
restraint? Yield to the wishes of others
without the least complaint?

Giving goals the green light and childish games
take the stop sign son, major altercation on
highway "I'm so Done", due to excessive
cerebral congestion, of emotion baggage bottle
necking the lanes of unrelieved tension,
halting levity and free thought in a dead lock of
major depression.

If no relief coming soon someone will blow a
head gasket.

In other words, take a vacation you workaholic
FREAK!!!
(Sorry, I typed that out loud.)

I'm
so
delirious!
A little space
please ...


Can't tell the difference between persistence or
passion desired, the heat of fervor stoked or
imagination inspired.

Whoa! Please excuse me head spinning with
ideas all attained, can't talk now in hot pursuits
that later can be explained.

Is this the end of the beginning?
Matters little as long as one is winning.
It's ok to be delirious with success.

What

is

your

composition?


What sweeping masterpiece is to be your legacy?
What sheet music will your life play from?
When will life 's opportunities ring their bell?
Which strategies are to beat their drum?
Where will your creativity and drive strum from?
Must keep making big sweeping accomplishments
with conductor's baton, yours is the big
movement, the captivating overture upon which
others can rock on.

Are your headlights on?


Beaming with *20/20* foresights? Don't drive thru
rough byways and highways of life without the
right insights.

Dark dangerous these times ahead, stay on well lit
and well paved paths with pragmatic tread.

Avoid potholes of importunity, observe all signs left
by those before us most dutifully.

Stay to the right, use nothing dim witted,
be safety conscious and properly outfitted.

# Keep dancing in the rain

Twirling, winding, bursting clouds soaked
with opportunity, a promenade between
spontaneous drops with impunity.

Sashay in the puddles rising from confident
expectation, remaining light, heated, and
nimble of feet replaces vanity and vexation.

Just a touch of heavenly dementia

Lost my thoughts in crowded star clusters,
my shoes in cumulonimbus cloud musters.
Heavy with ~ precipitations, lightning into
the heart of memory-lapsed altercations.

Who are you?

And don't you know I have heavenly detentions?
Don't worry as beyond a rainbow of doubt
haven't forgotten you in my starry memory
extensions.

Behold the ½ moon beauty

Fully awakened in celestial duty, how can one
not behold the ½ mooned beauty.

A luminary accompanying lofty dreams, so large,
almost touchable the crest at its radiant night beams.

Some creatures howl and roar at its behest,
others slumber through her regal station and
commanded to forget the rest.

For crying out loud! Even the moon gets its
beauty rest, Why don't you?

Way up we go


Rocket boosted dream fueled innovation,
rocketing thru the stratosphere to
achievement station, mission control;
all is a go for launch dissertation.

Ideas rising in minds zero gravity,
Internal visualization translations
to energized astrophysicality.

Keep reaching and
keep stretching as far as
big goals can take you.

# Why Is There Always Room For Improvement?

The Biggest Room in the world is not the
Sistine Chapel or Kennedy Space Center of
rocket boosted liftings, the unlimited space in
human potential to better express and expand
our siftings.

It's epicenter is to discover and grow our
talents unbounded, give shape and direction
to abilities well rounded.

If one is not growing daily in this space,
contraction is looming, and if one's skills,
though great, never get regular and proper
grooming,

Sad that full potential is not tapped as only
then it can be said that we never found that
massive room that's improving.

# ACKNOWLEDGED POETRY SOURCES

Poetry sources I would like to acknowledge:

Oprah's Book Club
Poetry (Magazine)
Poetryfoundation.org
Poetrysoup.com
Academy of American Poets
The Poetry Society of America
Poets & Writers, Inc
Duotrope
New Pages
The Marin Poetry Center
Poets House
The Science Fiction Poetry Association
PennSound
Dallas Poets Community
The Concord Poetry Center
Haiku Society of America
The Poetry Center of Chicago
Star*Line
National Federation of State Poetry Societies
Poetry Journals
Poetry Flash

Arsenic Lobster Poetry Journal
Smartish Pace
Ploughshares
Poet Lore
Poetry Superhighway
Nostrovia Poetry
Cordite Poetry Review
Tule Review
Up the Staircase Quarterly
Slipstream Magazine
Aberration Labyrinth
Plume
Parody
Now Culture
Aberration Labyrinth
The Hollins Critic
Iodine Poetry Journal
Lexicon Polaroid
Abramelin
The Rotary Dial
Chaparral
Blast Furnace
The Araya Review
U.S.1 Poets' Cooperative
Visions-International
Boxcar Poetry Review
My Favorite Bullet
The Innisfree Poetry Journal

Leveler
The Cape Rock
Rattle
32 Poems
491 Magazine
Antiphon Poetry Magazine
Free Verse: A Journal of Contemporary Poetry & Poetics
Exercise Bowler
Acorn: a Journal of Contemporary Haiku
The Michigan Poet
Toad the Journal
Found Poetry Review
Watermark: A Poet's Notebook
The Poetry Archive
Fishouse
Poetry Quarterly
Poetry Northwest
American Poetry Review
Library of Congress Poet Laureate
All Poetry Blogs
Verse Daily
The Page
The Columbia Granger's World of Poetry
Electronic Poetry Center
Poetry Daily
Button Poetry
Apples and Snakes
Kalamazoo Poetry Festival
Urbana Poetry Slam

Nuyorican Poets Café
Write Out Loud
Geraldine R. Dodge Poetry Program
Chicago Slam Works
The Performance Poetry Preservation Project
Winning Writers
Book That Poet
For Better for Verse
The Writer's Almanac with Garrison Keillor
American Life In Poetry
Wave Books Erasures Tool
Contemporary American Voices

# ABOUT THE AUTHOR

Robert C. Saunders has been a nurse in the Tampa Bay area for over 20 yrs. and is still expanding his horizons as a poet, author, songwriter, entrepreneur, marketer, and any other opportunities blown his way by winds of change.

Contact Robert at:
dynamicallyactivated@gmail.com

Visit the author website:
www.robertcsaunders.com
www.dynamicallyactivated.com

www.ingramcontent.com/pod-product-compliance
Lightning Source LLC
Chambersburg PA
CBHW032100080426
42733CB00006B/357